A Good Idea

by Lori Mortensen   illustrated by Julia Oliver

Cricket, Crow, and Owl lived in
the forest. It was a good place
to live except for one thing. They
all made so much noise that
they could not hear themselves.

2

One day, the noise was louder than ever. Finally Crow shouted, "Be quiet everyone! Stop being so rude!"

"You're the loudest of all," said Cricket.

"Me?" said Crow. "Everyone is so loud, I can't hear my bold caws."

"And who can hear my lovely chirps?" said Cricket. "Not me!"

"And who can hear my soft hoots?" said Owl. "Not me!"

The animals agreed they needed new rules.

"There are too many calls," said Crow. "Who will stop calling?"

"Everyone's too loud," said Cricket. "Who will whisper?"

"The forest is too small," said Owl. "Who will move away?"

Nobody liked these rules.
No one wanted to stop calling or move away.

"It's no good," said Crow. "We must think of something else."

The three animals thought and thought. Day turned into night.

"I know!" said Crow. "I will use the day to caw."

"And we will use the night to chirp and hoot," added Cricket and Owl.

They all agreed to try it.

And it was a good idea!